ANIMAL PREDATORS

Rattlesnakes

SANDRA MARKLE

LERNER PUBLICATIONS COMPANY / MINNEAPOLIS

The Animal World is Full of
PREDATORS.

Predators are the hunters that find, catch, and eat other animals—their prey—in order to survive. Every environment has its chain of hunters. The smaller, slower, less able predators become prey for the bigger, faster, more cunning hunters. And everywhere, there are just a few kinds of predators at the top of the food chain. *In the Americas from southern Canada through Argentina, this group of predators includes one or more kinds of rattlesnakes, like this black-tailed rattlesnake.*

One reason rattlesnakes are successful hunters is that—like this western rattlesnake—they are perfectly colored to hide from their prey. Then they can ambush it with a lightning-fast strike.

Rattlesnakes hunt at nearly any time of day or night, when it is warm enough. A snake needs to be warm to be active. It gets some of the heat its body needs from the food it eats. But this is not enough for the snake's muscles to work. Its body changes food into energy too slowly for that. Instead, a snake has to also soak up heat from the air and ground. As long as the air temperature is at least 60°F (15°C), a rattlesnake can warm itself enough to search for prey. It finds its prey using its keen sense of smell.

A rattlesnake has two ways to smell—through its nostrils and through a smell-sensing organ inside its mouth. A rattlesnake—like this Mojave rattlesnake—checks the air for scents every time it breathes. Its nasal cavity is packed with cells that detect scent matter in the air. It also checks for scents by flicking out its moist tongue.

The tongue picks up body oils or other bits of scent matter from the air, ground, rocks, or whatever else it touches. When the snake pulls its tongue back into its mouth, the twin tips brush against small bumps on the floor of its mouth. Muscles push these bumps up into a pair of pits on the roof of the snake's mouth. These pits, the Jacobson's organ, are also packed with scent-sensitive cells.

Snakes are carnivores, or meat eaters. Rattlesnakes eat mainly rodents, such as rats and mice. When this female timber rattlesnake goes hunting for prey, she travels in a fairly straight line until she detects a rodent's scent. Then she tracks this scent trail.

The scales covering her body act like an armor coat. They protect her from the prickly, sticky underbrush she's crawling through. The scales—like the ones shown in close-up here—are tough. They are made of the same material as claws, hooves, and fingernails. The stretchy skin in between the scales lets her coat flex as she moves. Sets of muscles hook the many ribs of her skeleton to bigger, wider scales on her belly. These muscles lift the belly scales, move them forward, and lower them again, pulling the snake along.

The female timber rattlesnake stops traveling when the scent of prey is very strong. She coils up next to a fallen branch and stays still. Her coloring helps her blend into her hiding place.

Minutes and then hours pass. Rattlesnakes are patient hunters. They are willing to wait several days before moving on. But this time, the female timber rattlesnake doesn't have to wait long. In just a few minutes, her prey, a mouse, comes close enough for her to see it. The rattlesnake can see with her eyes and with big heat-sensing pits between her nostrils and eyes.

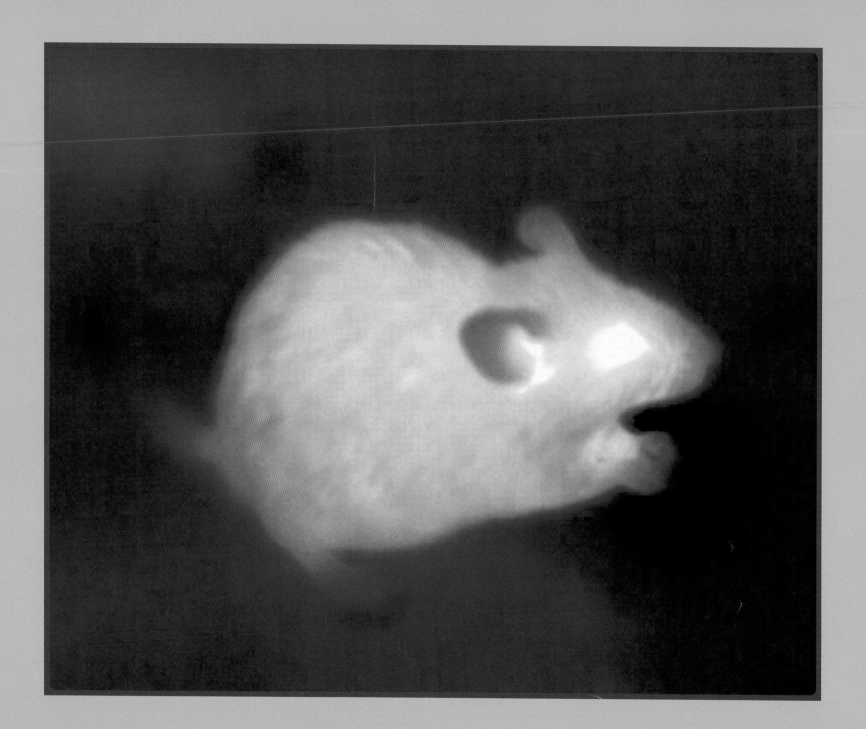

The rattlesnake's heat-sensing pits detect the mouse's shape. Cells in these pits detect differences in temperature as far as several body lengths away. At less than 1 foot (30 centimeters), the snake can sense even slight variations in temperature. A rattlesnake's ability to sense heat makes its prey stand out from the background. What the rattlesnake senses is similar to the image that heat-sensitive film captured of this mouse. This ability, called infrared vision, also helps the rattlesnake stay safe. A large heat shape could be a rattlesnake-eating predator, such as a coyote or a bobcat. When the rattlesnake's heat-sensing pits detect a big shape, the snake keeps still to blend in and hide.

The female timber rattlesnake also sees the mouse with her eyes. Because she has forward-facing eyes, she's able to judge exactly how far away the prey is. She holds the front part of her body in a loose S shape, which acts like a spring. As soon as the snake judges the deer mouse is within range, she straightens her neck with lightning speed. That propels her head forward. At the same instant, she opens her big mouth wide, and the fangs folded inside snap forward.

A rattlesnake's fangs have a hollow core with an opening at the sharp tip. When folded back inside its mouth, the fangs are enclosed in fleshy sheaths, or covers. As the rattlesnake bites, the fangs are pushed out of this covering. They puncture, or stab into, the prey and inject a little venom. The rattlesnake's venom is a mixture of poisonous chemicals and digestive juices. It is produced in glands just below the snake's eyes. This venom is another reason rattlesnakes are such successful predators. It lets them kill prey without a fight.

After she bites, the female timber rattlesnake pulls back her fangs and lets the deer mouse run away.

The rattlesnake's venom causes the deer mouse to bleed inside its body, and it dies minutes later. The rattlesnake flicks her tongue to collect the scent particles of the dead mouse. Once she finds it, she begins swallowing the mouse head first. This way the legs and ears fold back and go down more easily. Because all of a snake's teeth are sharp—it has no flat grinding teeth—the timber rattlesnake can't chew. She swallows her prey whole.

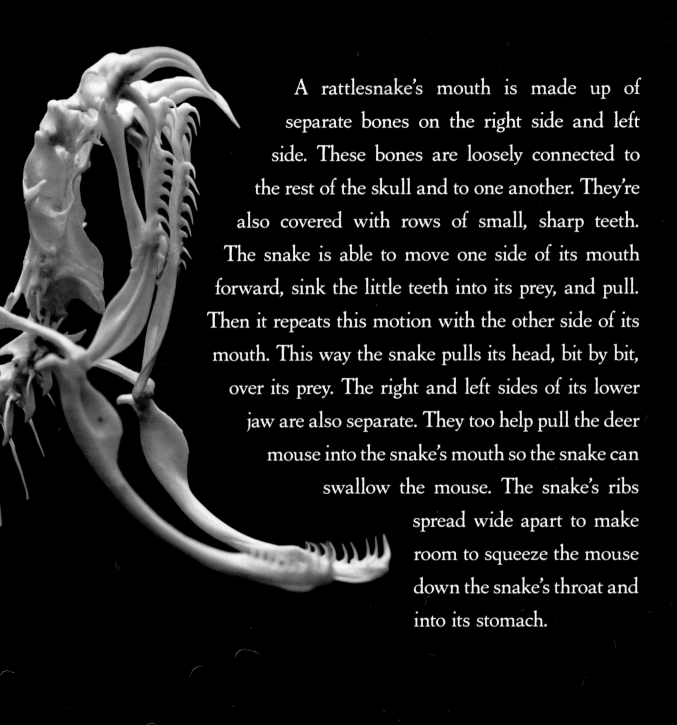

A rattlesnake's mouth is made up of separate bones on the right side and left side. These bones are loosely connected to the rest of the skull and to one another. They're also covered with rows of small, sharp teeth. The snake is able to move one side of its mouth forward, sink the little teeth into its prey, and pull. Then it repeats this motion with the other side of its mouth. This way the snake pulls its head, bit by bit, over its prey. The right and left sides of its lower jaw are also separate. They too help pull the deer mouse into the snake's mouth so the snake can swallow the mouse. The snake's ribs spread wide apart to make room to squeeze the mouse down the snake's throat and into its stomach.

The digestive juices in the female rattlesnake's venom break down its prey's tissues. The process begins the instant she bites. However, the snake may take more than a day to completely digest a mouse meal. For bigger prey, it may take several days. As long as the prey doesn't make too big a lump in the female timber rattlesnake's body, she keeps on crawling. Sometimes she starts hunting again, because it might take her days to find another meal. Usually, the snake eats about once a week. When prey is scarce, she may eat as few as six meals a year.

Today, the female timber rattlesnake takes time out to coil up and bask in the sunshine. Warming up helps her digest her food. Sometimes, if the day gets very warm or just to stay safe, a rattlesnake will coil up under a bush or a rock ledge. It will stick out just one loop—the part of its body containing its stomach—to soak up the sun's warmth.

Whether hunting or resting, rattlesnakes are constantly alert. Although they lack ears, they can sense vibrations. Even before this western diamondback rattlesnake smelled or saw the roadrunner, it felt this predator moving nearby. The rattlesnake could strike to defend itself. But when attacking a bigger predator, it risks getting hurt in the struggle. It sends a warning instead. Rattlesnakes have a built-in alarm, a rattle, at the end of their tails. They use this to warn enemies to stay away. When the roadrunner comes close, the rattlesnake sticks its tail up and shakes its rattle.

The rattlesnake's rattle forms as the snake sheds its skin. Crawling around is hard on a snake's scaly skin. A rattlesnake sheds and replaces the outer layer two or three times a year. As it sheds its skin, the last bit of the old skin stays stuck to the tail end of its body. After shedding several times, a rattlesnake has bits of old skin, like a stack of paper cups, at the tip of its tail. The more times it sheds, the longer its rattle becomes until some segments break off.

To warn off the roadrunner, the diamondback rattlesnake shakes the tip of its tail back and forth as fast as sixty times a second. The segments bump into one another to make a startling buzz.

As the rattlesnake starts to strike, the roadrunner flaps its wings and leaps. The bird escapes being bitten and goes in search of easier prey. The rattlesnake keeps on hunting too.

A rattlesnake usually has a home range, an area in which it regularly hunts. This female western diamondback crawls across familiar ground and into a river that crosses her range. She moves her body from side to side so her belly scales push against the water. In this way, she swims toward a place where she has caught prey before.

Still, she has a long wait before a wood rat finally comes close enough to catch. This will be the rattlesnake's last meal for some time. The nights are starting to get cooler, and the days are taking much longer to warm up.

To escape freezing temperatures, snakes—like western diamondback rattlesnakes—move underground. They often crawl to the same winter den year after year. Young rattlesnakes follow the scent of other rattlesnakes to find a den for their first winter. The den may be a hole under a rock outcrop. It may be a burrow that a badger or other animal has left. Sometimes hundreds of the same kind of rattlesnake, like these western diamondbacks, will den together.

In the den, the snake's heart rate, or number of heartbeats per minute, slows. The snake sleeps, wakes to move a little, and sleeps some more. It uses so little food energy, it doesn't need to hunt. When the weather warms again, the snakes crawl out of the den.

Some kinds of rattlesnakes mate right before or after denning, when they are close together. Others—like speckled rattlesnakes—need to hunt first. It's late summer before the female speckled rattlesnake is ready to mate. Like all female rattlesnakes, she announces her readiness by giving off pheromones, a scented chemical. The scent attracts male speckled rattlesnakes.

These two males are wrestling for a nearby female. They push each other until one male pushes the other's head to the ground. The loser glides off. The winner joins the female in a swaying, twining courtship dance. When the pair finally mates, the male transfers his sperm, male reproductive cells, into the female's body. The female will store the sperm in her body until she ovulates, or produces egg cells.

Timber rattlesnakes most often mate in the fall, before denning. But it's too cold during the winter months for young snakes to develop. The female timber rattlesnakes store the males' sperm over the winter and ovulate in the spring after they leave their den. When a sperm cell merges with an egg cell, a baby snake begins to develop.

Even though she has not eaten since last fall, the pregnant female timber rattlesnake doesn't go hunting. Instead, she finds a place to bask and soak up the sun's heat. Just as a bird sits on its eggs to keep them warm, the female timber rattlesnake warms herself. The warmth helps the babies inside her grow. Because there aren't a lot of good basking sites, pregnant female timber rattlesnakes often bask together.

Inside its mother, each baby rattlesnake is enclosed in its thin, clear egg. The baby gets the food energy it needs from the yolk ball that's attached to it. Just before birth, a baby rattlesnake absorbs any yolk that's left. This will be its only food until it catches its first prey. A baby rattlesnake is born when the female—like this South American rattlesnake— pushes her offspring, one by one, out of her body.

As soon as they're born, baby rattlesnakes—like these timber rattlesnakes—push on their thin egg covering to break it open. Only about 10 inches (25 cm) long, the babies look like small versions of their parents. They're also already producing venom.

Newborn rattlesnakes aren't ready to hunt, though. They won't be ready for about ten days. They have to shed their skin first. Even though it's been nearly ten months since she's eaten, the mother timber rattlesnake stays with her brood until then. Staying nearby, she protects her young from predators, such as red-tailed hawks and coyotes. These predators are less likely to attack an adult rattlesnake. The other female timber rattlesnakes also stay nearby with their broods. It's safer yet to be part of a group of rattlesnakes.

When the baby rattlesnake is finally ready to shed its skin, its eyes become cloudy. Its old skin, even the gogglelike covering over its eyes, begins to separate from the new skin underneath. Soon the youngster rubs its nose on anything rough enough to break open the old skin. Then the little snake catches the loose skin on something, like a twig or a bit of rock, and crawls forward. The old baby skin peels off. The pre-button at the end of its tail also snaps off, leaving behind a bit of its first baby skin—the beginning of its rattle.

One by one, the mother timber rattlesnake's eight youngsters crawl away. Finally, she can go hunting again. She needs to hunt to store up enough food energy to be ready to den when winter comes once again. It will be at least a year, perhaps several years, before she builds up enough food energy to be ready to produce more young.

Meanwhile, each of the eight young timber rattlesnakes in this year's brood is on its own. They may hunt and catch prey before they den for the first time, or they may wait until they emerge from the den in the spring. But whenever they start, another generation of rattlesnakes will be on the hunt.

Looking Back

- Compare the eyes of the rattlesnakes on pages 11 and 16 to see how they change in bright and dim light. In bright light, the pupils—the opening that lets light enter the eyes—narrows to a slit. In dim light, the pupils open wide.

- Take another look at the striking timber rattlesnake on page 14. Check out the protective covering that surrounds its sharp fangs when its mouth is closed.

- Look closely at the western diamondback rattlesnake on page 25. You can see how the snake's elastic skin stretches to help it swallow such big prey.

- Look back at the rattlesnake giving birth on page 32. Can you tell its age by counting its rattles? If you need a clue, reread the text on page 20.

Glossary

CARNIVORE: animal that eats only other animals

EGG: female reproductive cell; also the name given to the structure in which a baby develops

FANG: sharp tooth used to inject venom into the snake's prey

HOME RANGE: an area where an animal lives and hunts

JACOBSON'S ORGAN: smell-sensing organ in the roof of a rattlesnake's mouth

OVULATE: to produce egg cells

PHEROMONE: a chemical produced by a female animal, signaling its readiness to mate and reproduce

PREDATOR: an animal that hunts other animals

PREY: an animal that a predator catches to eat

RATTLE: a stack of hard skin segments at the end of a rattlesnake's tail. Rattlesnakes shake their rattles to warn away predators.

SCALE: flat, hard plates that protect a snake's skin

SPERM: male reproductive cell

VENOM: poison a snake injects in its prey when it bites

YOLK: food supply for a baby that develops in an egg

Further Information

Books

Arnosky, Jim. *All About Rattlesnakes.* New York: Scholastic, 1997. Investigate rattlesnake anatomy. Paintings bring the facts to life.

Feldman, Heather. *Diamondbacks.* The Really Wild Life of Snakes series. New York: Rosen Publishing Group, 2004. Learn about the lives of diamondback rattlesnakes.

Lavies, Bianca. *The Secretive Timber Rattlesnake.* New York: Dutton Juvenile Books, 1990. Close-up photos and text combine to show the life of the timber rattlesnake.

Markle, Sandra. *Outside and Inside Snakes.* New York: Aladdin, 1998. Explore a snake's body, inside and out, and see how it lives.

Websites

Rattlesnake Museum
http://www.rattlesnakes.com
Take a virtual trip to the American International Rattlesnake Museum. Learn about different kinds of rattlesnakes.

San Diego Zoo: Rattlesnakes
http://www.sandiegozoo.org/animalbytes/t-rattlesnake.html
Visit the zoo on the Web to find out amazing facts about rattlesnakes. See photos of rattlesnakes and listen to a Mojave rattlesnake's rattle.

Western Diamondback Rattlesnake
http://whozoo.org/AnlifeSS2001/mindpapr/MP_ WesternDiamondback.html
Learn more about the largest kind of rattlesnake in North America.

Index

For Dr. Harry Greene in appreciation for his research and conservation efforts

The author would like to thank the following people for sharing their expertise and enthusiasm: Dr. Rulon Clark, San Diego State University; and Dr. Harry W. Greene, Cornell University. The author would also like to express a special thank-you to Skip Jeffery for his help and support during the creative process.

Photo Acknowledgments

The images in this book are used with the permission of: © Bianca Lavies/National Geographic/Getty Images, pp. 1, 35; © Dag Sundberg/The Image Bank/Getty Images, p. 3; © A. Cosmos Blank/Photo Researchers, Inc., p. 4; © David A. Northcott/CORBIS, pp. 7, 8; © Peter B. Kaplan/Photo Researchers, Inc., p. 9 (main); © Albert Lleal/Minden Pictures, p. 9 (inset); © Mark MacEwen/Oxford Scientific/Photolibrary, p. 11; © Edward Kinsman/Photo Researchers, Inc., p. 12; © E. R. Degginger/Photo Researchers, Inc., p. 14; © Joe McDonald, pp. 15, 16; REUTERS/Victor Fraile, p. 17; © John Cancalosi/naturepl.com, pp. 19, 23, 25, 31, 34; © Joe McDonald/CORBIS, p. 21; © Tom Bean/Stone/Getty Images, p. 22; © David Welling/naturepl.com, p. 24; © Joel Sartore/National Geographic/Getty Images, p. 26; © Rupert Barrington/naturepl.com, p. 29; © Daniel Heuclin/NHPA/Photoshot, p. 32; © Zigmund Leszczynski/Animals Animals, p. 33; © Mary Ann McDonald, p. 37.

Cover: © Joel Sartore/National Geographic/Getty Images.

Lerner Publications Company
A division of Lerner Publishing Group, Inc.
241 First Avenue North
Minneapolis, MN 55401 U.S.A.

Website address: www.lernerbooks.com

Websites listed in Further Reading are current at time of publication.

Library of Congress Cataloging-in-Publication Data

Markle, Sandra.
    Rattlesnakes / by Sandra Markle.
        p.   cm. — (Animal predators)
    Includes bibliographical references and index.
    ISBN 978–1–58013–539–9 (lib. bdg. : alk. paper)
    1. Rattlesnakes—Juvenile literature. I. Title.
QL666.O69M345 2010
597.96'38—dc22   2008038038

Manufactured in the United States of America
1 2 3 4 5 6 – DP – 15 14 13 12 11 10